Dear

Th[...]
care of [...] mommy
was gone. I had fun with
you even though you put
water over my head.

Love,
   Brady
(and mommy)

My Dad MADE A DIFFERENCE

Photography by

KATHLEEN FRANCOUR

HARVEST HOUSE PUBLISHERS
Eugene, Oregon

MY DAD MADE A DIFFERENCE

Text Copyright © 2001 by Focus on the Family®
Published by Harvest House Publishers
Eugene, Oregon 97402

Focus on the Family, headed by Dr. James Dobson, is an organization that reaches families with the message of God's love. Focus on the Family® is a registered trademark of Focus on the Family, Colorado Springs, CO 80995. For more information, please contact:

    Focus on the Family
    Colorado Springs, CO 80995
    1-800-A-Family (232–6459)
    www.family.org

Library of Congress Cataloging-in-Publication Data
Focus on the Family/ My dad made a difference : the heritage of a faithful father / photography by Kathleen Francour.
    p. cm.
    ISBN 0-7369-0551-0
    1.Fathers. 2.Fatherhood--Religious aspects--Christianity. 1.Francour, Kathleen.

    HQ756 .M84 2001

                                          00-047130

Kathleen Francour's hand-tinted photographs reflect the old-fashioned values of home, family, love, loyalty, and friendship. The photography in this book is copyrighted by Kathleen Francour and may not be used without permission of the photographer. For more information, please contact:

    Kathleen Francour Photography & Design
    P.O. Box 1206
    Carefree, AZ 85377

Photographic printing by Isgo Lepejian

Design and production by Koechel Peterson and Associates, Minneapolis, Minnesota

Harvest House Publishers has made every effort to trace the ownership of all poems and quotes. In the event of a question arising from the use of a poem or quote, we regret any error made and will be pleased to make the necessary correction in future editions of this book.

Acknowledgments

"A Faithful Giant," copyright © by Lynda Hunter. Used by permission.
"In Everything Give Thanks," copyright © by Ann Hibbard. Used by permission.
"A Lesson in Love," copyright © by Tom Wagoner. Used by permission.
"When Dad Turned the Bicycle Loose," copyright © by Cliff Schimmels. Used by permission.

Scripture quotations are taken from the Holy Bible, New International Version®, Copyright © 1973, 1978, 1984 by the International Bible Society. Used by permission of Zondervan Publishing House. Verses marked KJV are taken from the King James Version of the Bible.

Printed in Italy

01 02 03 04 05 06 07 08 09 10 / PBI / 10 9 8 7 6 5 4 3 2 1

BLESSED INDEED IS THE
MAN WHO HEARS
MANY GENTLE VOICES
CALL HIM FATHER!

Lydia M. Child

A FAITHFUL GIANT

The late afternoon rays of the autumn sun lay warm upon my hair as I played with my truck in the sand. Suddenly, I heard footsteps rustling through the leaves. A long shadow appeared as my dad reached out with both arms and scooped me up, up, up into the air and crushed me with a hug.

Dad began to sing "Jesus Loves Me, This I Know" as we set out for our daily walk to visit the black-and-white cows across the road. His walk was not swift, but I loved the gentle sway of his giant stride that brought us there quickly. The cows stared with their customary curiosity as they continued to chew their cud. Dad told me how the cows searched carefully

for good grazing but quickly returned to the barn when the master called.

One day when I was 7, my dad played ball with me in the yard. The trees were our bases. No matter where I made my pitch, Dad was able to extend his great arms and make contact with his bat. When I retrieved the ball, he slowed down and pretended to be surprised as I tagged him out and we fell laughing into the grass.

Dad taught my teenage Sunday school class. He stood tall as he shared his great knowledge and showed us the way to the cross and to a life with Jesus. I sometimes talked and fooled around with my friends and failed to listen to what Dad told us. But I saw a consistency in what he said and what I saw him do as he studied his Bible each night and knelt beside his bed in prayer.

As I matured, I watched others also see the giant in my dad. They called him often for prayer and counsel. Many times I heard him return just in time to go to his job after ministering to someone through the night.

As a man, I traveled one day to be

> IT BEHOOVES THE FATHER TO BE VIRTUOUS WHO DESIRES HIS SON TO BE MORE VIRTUOUS THAN HE HAS BEEN.
> *Plautus*

with my dad at his bedside. It was hard for me to see this giant sick and unable to do all the things I remembered. *What is Dad's secret*, I wondered, *to being so big? Why doesn't he topple as so many other great men have? How has he managed to remain a spiritual giant?*

I walked toward his room but stopped at his door as I heard him pray.

"…and Lord, for Mary. She needs a touch on her body as she undergoes this surgery. Be with my children, each and every one of them, as they face decisions they must make. And God, make me a faithful servant. Draw me closer to be more like You."

I walked into the room. His eyes filled with tears, and a weak smile touched his lips. Giant arms stretched out feebly to

embrace me. We talked. We cried. Then Dad slept.

As he did, I reached over to his side and picked up his Bible. It was open to a page that was clearly marked. "But I keep under my body, and bring it into subjection: lest that by any means, when I have preached to others, I myself should be a castaway" (1 Corinthians 9:27, KJV).

I looked at my dad's labored breathing and suddenly I knew his secret. He was a

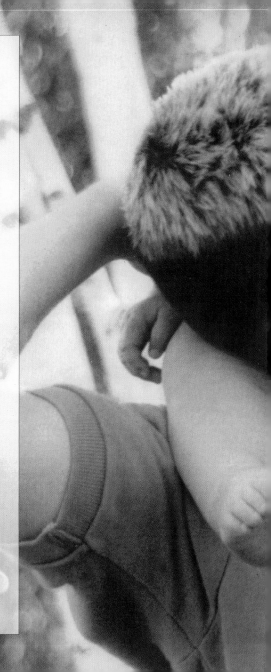

giant who was still growing. He daily measured himself by standing next to God, where anyone appears small. He continued to search out better pasture and responded dutifully to the Master, like the cows he once described. He opened himself so God could make him better at all he did. And he devoted himself to Bible reading and prayer, the most fertile grounds in which to grow.

Dad never woke from his sleep that afternoon but passed on to be with his Lord. As I walked from his room into the cool spring air, I realized God had been building the inner part of my dad even up to the hour he died. That was what made him a giant.

—LYNDA HUNTER,
as written from her brother
Phillip's perspective

A FATHER'S PRAYER

Dear God, my little boy of three
Has said his nightly prayer to Thee;
Before his eyes were closed to sleep,
He asked that Thou his soul would keep.
And I, still kneeling at his bed,
My hand upon his tousled head,
Do ask with deep humility,
That Thou, dear Lord, remember me.
Make me, kind Lord, a worthy Dad,
That I may lead this little lad
In pathways ever fair and bright,
That I may keep his steps aright.
O God, his trust must never be
Destroyed or even marred by me.
So, for the simple things he prayed
With childish voice so unafraid,
I, trembling, ask the same from Thee.
Dear Lord, kind Lord, remember me.

ANONYMOUS

SOWING SEEDS OF FAITH

I grew up in the home of a pastor in a pioneer mission field. At the time, I didn't really understand how blessed I was. Many know my father as the author of *Experiencing God,* Henry Blackaby, but to me he is just Dad! His spiritual guidance set the pace in our family of what it meant to walk with God.

My early years were very formative, helping me understand the nature of faith in practical terms. But that didn't mean that I always liked it. You see, it was one thing for Dad to follow the Lord and sacrifice for the Kingdom's sake, but I didn't have a choice in the matter. Dad *chose* to be a pastor; I was *drafted* into the role of being a pastor's son. From a child's perspective, that meant that we were poor. It meant that I had to go to church twice on Sunday and Prayer Meeting on Wednesday night. It meant

AS EARLY AS I CAN REMEMBER ANYTHING, I REMEMBER WALKING INTO HIS STUDY AND FINDING HIM PRAYING. THAT COMMUNICATES IT STARTS AT THE TOP WITH GOD, THROUGH MY PARENTS, TO ME AND ONE DAY IT WILL JUST BE ME AND GOD.

Andy Stanley

that I was an "ex-officio" member of all children's activities. Furthermore, it meant that my father imposed a standard of morality that was different than my friends were living. As a 12-year-old boy, I had a lot to live up to.

Even though I had to endure the challenges of being the preacher's kid, I would not trade it for anything. It instilled in me that there was a God—I saw Him every day. My father had a conviction:

"Take your faith to your children, and your problems to God." He always talked positively about the Lord. He would talk about the mighty acts of God during mealtime. He would share how God answered prayer. Our home became a safe refuge in a difficult world. I cannot recall a time when my father complained or felt sorry for himself. He never talked negatively about the church. I know he had difficult days, but he did not lay his burdens on his children; he took them to the Lord. As a result, we all learned to take our burdens to the Lord and find the provision of God.

During my years of searching, I cannot remember my father telling me what I ought to do with my life; he just pointed me to the Lord. I, therefore, have not followed my father's footsteps, but

the footsteps of my Lord. Funny thing, those steps have led me to the pastorate!

Thanks, Dad, for not telling me the way, but for pointing me to Christ, who is the Way, the Truth, and the Life.

—MEL BLACKABY

A Father IS MANY THINGS TO HIS CHILD. AS A TEACHER, HE HELPS US LEARN VALUABLE LESSONS ABOUT GOD'S LAW AND PURPOSES. AS A GUIDE, HE SETS A PATTERN FOR LIFE—FOR THE IDEALS WE SHOULD EMBRACE AND THE GOALS WE SHOULD SEEK. AS A COMPANION, HE PROVIDES THAT CLOSE FRIENDSHIP GOD WISHES EVERY YOUNG PERSON TO ENJOY. IT IS, INDEED, THROUGH THE INFLUENCE OF A FATHER ON EARTH THAT WE BETTER KNOW AND UNDERSTAND OUR FATHER IN HEAVEN.

James Keller

A LESSON IN LOVE

The 19th-century lamp stood proudly on the living room end table, a crown jewel in an otherwise plain household. To Dad, it was a mother pearl—the one priceless object in a home of hand-me-down furnishings.

The lamp had been passed down through my father's family for generations. Before the turn of the century, it had been an oil lamp, sporting a large, aqua crystal-ball globe and a gold-painted, ornamental steel base. At some point, a family member must have adapted it to electricity.

The lamp's shade made you think you were in the middle of a mountain forest with its awesome scene of woods and

18

waterfalls. It was one of the most beautiful things I'd ever seen.

Dad took great pride in showing the lamp to all our visitors, carefully detailing its long family history. That lamp not only lit our home, but brought light to my dad's heart. It also taught me an important lesson about life.

One day, when my brother and I were young, we were roughhousing in the living room. He was the cowboy, and I was his bucking bronco. Cowboys have ropes, you know, so to tame this wild bronc, he lassoed me. Then he tied me to the tall end table that displayed the Wagoner family lamp.

The bronco reared. The rope grew taut. The table tipped over, and the priceless heirloom came crashing to the floor.

I remember the look of horror on Mom's face when she came running and found the shattered crystal globe on the thin and worn rug.

Instantly, my brother and I started crying. We had broken the most precious possession of the most precious man we knew. Our anguish grew into fear as Mom, with tears in her eyes, cleaned up the broken pieces. She tenderly put the large shards of broken glass and the crinkled lamp shade in a box, as if somehow God would heal it through the skilled hands of a miracle craftsman. But that would never happen. You can't glue together slivers of glass.

Mom scolded us for our carelessness, and she warned us of the consequences when Dad got home. My brother and I knew we deserved a punishment. We cowered in our rooms, wishing over and over that we could turn back the clock and make the lamp whole again.

The lesson from my father on that awful yet wonderful day was a lesson of love and forgiveness. Dad taught me that his family was more precious than his physical possessions, even his best ones. I was reminded of this when Jesus said in Matthew 6:19-21: "Do not store up for yourselves treasures on earth, where moth and rust [and boys] destroy, and where thieves break in and steal. But store up for yourselves treasures in heaven, where moth and rust do not destroy, and where thieves do not break in and steal. For where your treasure is, there your heart will be also" (bracketed material added by author).

> IT IS THE WISE FATHER WHO KNOWS THAT THE MOST IMPORTANT THINGS IN LIFE AREN'T THINGS.
>
> *Anonymous*

Another passage that spoke to me was: "Therefore, there is now no condemnation for those who are in Christ Jesus...The Spirit himself testifies with our spirit that we are God's children" (Romans 8:1,16).

There was no condemnation that day I broke the family lamp, though I deserved it. My father's love and forgiveness were greater than the value of his prized possession. And today, when our children tip over lamps, wreck the family car, forget their promises, or break our hearts, how I react will stick with them for a long time. Perhaps for eternity.

These days, my wife, Brenda, and I enjoy browsing through antique stores, looking out for a family lamp similar to the one I broke. My father is 73, and it would give me the greatest pleasure to find a lamp just like the one he loved. I doubt I'll find a replica, but that's all right. I experienced the real thing—a father's love—and that's something neither of us will ever be able to fix with a price tag.

—TOM WAGONER

AS A FATHER HAS COMPASSION

ON HIS CHILDREN, SO THE LORD

HAS COMPASSION ON THOSE

WHO FEAR HIM.

The Book of Psalms

PRAYER FOR A DAUGHTER

Mold me a daughter, O Lord, who will

Be patient in the face of trials

And humble in the hour of triumph;

One who will exalt, and never belittle,

Who will forgive, and never begrudge.

Mold me a daughter whose heart will be

Always open to those who need her love,

Whose hands will be always willing to

Soothe and comfort, to help and heal.

Give her enough of the sunshine of

Laughter to dry away the mists of sorrow,

And enough high courage to cheerfully

Complete each task that must be done.

Mold me a daughter who will give of

Herself that she may gain the knowledge

Of how to live, who will not mourn that

Life's roses have thorns, but rejoice

That Life's thorns have roses.

Then I, her father, will declare, "The

World is richer by one lovely soul."

George Webster Douglas

IN *E*VERYTHING, GIVE THANKS

*M*y father and I frequently went for long walks in the woods behind our house. Dad is a lover of beauty, a poet at heart, and he frequently quoted the famous writer Robert Frost to express his wonder at God's creation. His enthusiasm was contagious. Thus, I developed a deep love of nature, too, taking my own children for walks in the woods. If my father could pass his love of nature on to me so simply, surely we as parents can pass a grateful heart on to our children.

When all is said and done, only the Lord can plant the seed of gratitude in children's hearts. We can do our part by remembering that the kids are watching our actions and will imitate us. That is why we need to weave thanksgiving into the fabric of our lives. As parents, we have to set the pace for expressing appreciation in the home.

—ANN HIBBARD

LITTLE EYES UPON YOU

THERE *are little eyes upon you*
and they're watching night and day.
There are little ears that quickly
take in every word you say.
There are little hands all eager
to do anything you do;
And a little boy who's dreaming
of the day he'll be like you.
You're the little fellow's idol,
you're the wisest of the wise.
In his little mind about you
no suspicions ever rise.

He believes in you devoutly,
holds all you say and do;
He will say and do in your way
when he's grown up just like you.
There's a wide-eyed little fellow
who believes you're always right;
and his eyes are always opened,
and he watches day and night.
You are setting an example
every day in all you do;
For the little boy who's waiting
to grow up to be like you.

AUTHOR UNKNOWN

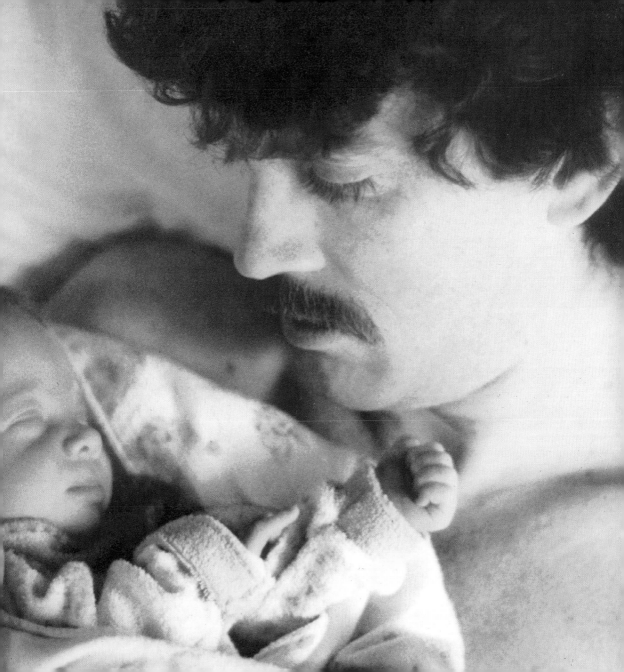

FOR *E*XAMPLE

*F*athers lead by example. There's always a small child watching—just as I did—establishing a foundation on which to build his future.

While I was growing up, my father didn't say much about his past. So I watched his actions—for me they clearly marked the faithful course he had chosen to set his life on.

I can recall him saying on a few occasions, "I could have worked 16 hours a day, and we could have had a much larger house and had more money and things. But before I married your mother, I made some decisions about how I was going to spend my time and money." Dad did work hard, and we

had a roomy house and plenty to eat. But what I remember now is that he was there to share that house and food with us. It was rare that he walked in the door for dinner later than 6:00 P.M. Because of his constant example, it never occurred to us that he would have wanted it to be otherwise.

We always knew that Dad had put himself in 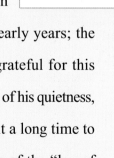 God's hands during his early years; the four of us children are grateful for this above all else. But because of his quietness, sometimes we had to wait a long time to find out other particulars of the "lay of the land" that had shaped Dad's life.

His road started out in a valley that was hard to get out of. Like many young men who had grown up during the Depression having known lack, he was disposed to value the security that money and things seem to bring. After training as a navy officer during World War II and then moving to Oregon to finish his schooling on the GI Bill, Dad was set to cut a swath in life.

Along with a group of other young men, he was hired and trained by one of the big oil companies and posted abroad— in the Philippines.

Over the next couple years, though,

he began to be disturbed by something. He'd been watching the lives of other Americans who worked with him, and he saw signs that their lives were fraying at the edges while becoming emptier in the center. Indulgence wasn't taking them anywhere.

Dad returned to the United States for a visit, then decided he wasn't going to continue his path abroad. While he was sorting things out and finding work back in Oregon, he was introduced to a young woman from Seattle. The next year she became his wife and life companion on the new course that God was setting for him—and the two of them.

> THESE COMMANDMENTS THAT I GIVE YOU TODAY ARE TO BE UPON YOUR HEARTS. IMPRESS THEM ON YOUR CHILDREN. TALK ABOUT THEM WHEN YOU SIT AT HOME AND WHEN YOU WALK ALONG THE ROAD, WHEN YOU LIE DOWN AND WHEN YOU GET UP.
>
> *The Book of Deuteronomy*

So what marks has Dad left on the trail that he's now followed for nearly 50 years? The marks, the impressions, are mostly in the lives of other people—like me. All of those marks have taken time to make, and he has had the time to make them because of the road he's followed.

Among many things, Dad has put the stamp of "enough" onto my heart. "Enough" says "The money and things God has given me are *enough* to work out

33

FOR EXAMPLE

His aims for my life right now." Because Dad has walked through married life wanting only *enough,* I have never seen him stumble because he was striving for money. When my wife and I decided to buy a different house a few months ago, we reckoned on the following: Will the upkeep of the house and yard allow our time to be freer for our family and the people in God's family? Is it a house that is better fitted for having guests than our old one? (I recall many dinner guests and overnight guests from my younger years. Dad loves to see people be comfortable and enjoy themselves.) Will the mortgage payments overburden us, causing worry and stealing our time? Will we be content here for the future—in other words, will we allow this house to be *enough* for us? All those questions were rooted in

my observations of my father's life.

The decades Dad has been my example—the years he's spent preparing for early-morning Bible studies with other men, or studying to bring a message on Sunday to our church fellowship, or guarding himself from "opportunities" that would have taken him away from us, his family—have left behind a road for me to travel.

34

Some undiscerning people may call the road my father chose a rut. I call it a trail—a well-trodden, heavily blazed path, a path with a clear direction. It's a path that many other men have been drawn to by the example of his sure and steady steps. It's a path from which Dad can nearly sight his goal—to be at the side of Jesus.

And as I look at my own life, my own family—what I do with my abilities, my money, my time—it's a path that I find myself wanting to choose more and more.

—PAUL GOSSARD

GOD TOOK THE STRENGTH OF A MOUNTAIN,

THE MAJESTY OF A TREE,

THE WARMTH OF A SUMMER SUN,

THE CALM OF A QUIET SEA,

THE GENEROUS SOUL OF NATURE,

THE COMFORTING ARM OF NIGHT,

THE WISDOM OF THE AGES,

THE POWER OF THE EAGLE'S FLIGHT,

THE JOY OF A MORNING IN SPRING,

THE FAITH OF A MUSTARD SEED,

THE PATIENCE OF ETERNITY,

THE DEPTH OF A FAMILY NEED.

THEN GOD COMBINED THESE QUALITIES.

WHEN THERE WAS NOTHING MORE TO ADD,

HE KNEW HIS MASTERPIECE WAS COMPLETE,

AND SO, HE CALLED IT..."DAD!"

—Author Unknown

35

BE KIND TO THY FATHER,

FOR WHEN THOU WERT YOUNG,

WHO LOVED THEE SO FONDLY AS HE?

HE CAUGHT THE FIRST ACCENTS

THAT FELL FROM THY TONGUE,

AND JOINED IN THY INNOCENT GLEE.

Margaret Courtney

PA ALWAYS LAUGHED OUT
LOUD AND HIS LAUGH WAS
LIKE GREAT BELLS RINGING.

Laura Ingalls Wilder
LITTLE HOUSE ON THE PRAIRIE

BUILD ME A SON

O Lord, who will be strong enough to know when he is weak and brave enough to face himself when he is afraid, one who will be proud and unbending in honest defeat and humble and gentle in victory.

Build me a son whose wishes will not take the place of deeds, a son who knows Thee—and that to know himself is the foundation of knowledge.

Lead him, I pray, not in the path of ease and comfort, but under the stress and spur of difficulties and challenge. Here let him learn to stand up to the storm, here let him learn compassion for those who fail.

Build me a son whose heart will be clean, whose goal will be high, a son who will master himself before he seeks to master other men, one who will reach into the future, yet never forget the past. And after all these things are his, add, I pray, enough of a sense of humor so that he may always be serious yet never take himself too seriously. Give him humility, so that he may always remember the simplicity of true greatness, the open mind of true wisdom, and the meekness of true strength. Then I, his father, will dare to whisper, "I have not lived in vain."

GENERAL DOUGLAS MACARTHUR

39

AND HE GOT UP AND

CAME TO HIS FATHER.

BUT WHILE HE WAS

STILL A LONG WAY OFF,

HIS FATHER SAW HIM,

AND FELT COMPASSION

FOR HIM, AND RAN

AND EMBRACED HIM,

AND KISSED HIM.

The Book of Luke

WHEN DAD TURNED THE BICYCLE LOOSE

*H*ockaday Hardware sold more than hardware. One day I was walking by the store without thought of needing anything when I spotted it. Right in the middle of the window as a shameless invitation to lust and envy was a red and white bicycle with all the trimmings—large fenders, mud flaps, reflector, whitewall tires, and handlebar grips with leather straps. I knew immediately that I had to own that bicycle.

Getting my mom and dad to see the urgency of owning the bike became a major challenge. I had two strategic options. First, I could use the divide-and-conquer technique. This meant catching them one at a time and starting my conversation on

the positive: "Momma said that it was all right with her for me to have that bicycle if it was all right with you." That worked on less-than-life-threatening urgencies, such as sleeping over with a friend. But the bicycle issue was too serious to be treated with any form of trickery.

The second option was the direct approach; just ask them. This seemed more logical. I found my parents sitting in the living room after supper, so I presented my case. I shall never forget their conversation. Mom was the first one to join the cause. As she tried to persuade my dad, he asked a leading question: "Do you think the bicycle would improve his behavior?"

"No," Mom said with a sigh, "but it should distribute it around on a little wider scale." With that, the deal was sealed.

Dad had to go get the beauty by himself, because there wouldn't have been room for both me and the bicycle in the back seat. In those days, bicycles were major chunks of iron and steel.

As I waited out in the yard all morning for Dad's return, I wondered what could be keeping him so long. I found myself hoping that if he had had a wreck, there wouldn't be any damage to the bike, regardless of any other pain that might be incurred. Finally, after a very long morning passed, Dad came home, and I helped him unload.

Then I had a major life lesson. You don't just hop on a bike and go pedaling off into the sunset. You have to master it, and that requires attention, mental skill, and physical dexterity. I was deficient in at least two of these.

I went to work learning how to ride a bike. My dad demonstrated for me. He explained and held it up while I tried it, but nothing worked. I took one spill after another, always cautious to dent myself instead of the bike. I cried myself to sleep, not because I was skinned and bruised, but because I had become convinced that I would never master the art of bicycle riding. I was destined to live an impoverished life.

One evening my dad came home and urged me out to the road for another lesson. And something happened. Just as we had done a hundred times before, he held the bike by the back fender and ran along as

ONE FATHER IS WORTH MORE THAN A HUNDRED SCHOOLMASTERS.
English Proverb

I pedaled. But this time it was different. He turned loose, and I was actually riding on my own—traveling down the road at a high rate of speed.

I have no idea what it is going to be like in that great moment when I cross over to spend eternity with Jesus; but I think it might be just like that moment Dad turned the bike loose. I will realize I am better than I ever thought I was at things I never thought I could do.

In His wonderful process of creation, God gave me talent and skill and ability. But I didn't know it in the beginning. I just lived my life thinking I couldn't accomplish anything. Then one day, Dad turned me loose. I became the parent I never thought I could be. I hit a singing note I never thought I could reach. I made a speech I never thought I could make.

How awesome when I finally understood that the Creator had equipped me for more than I ever gave Him credit.

My dad turned the bicycle loose, and that was one of the biggest lessons of my life.

—CLIFF SCHIMMELS

Why God Made Fathers

God made Fathers
to work and play.
God made Fathers
to sing and pray.

Who would whistle
those merry tunes
Of Yankee Doodle or
Old Zip Coon?

Who would guide
in gentle ways
Strengthen, care for
all one's days?

He was made to
build things strong
And to romp and grow
within right and wrong.

God made Fathers
to love pets and their wonders,
To help you with homework,
like sets and numbers.

And indeed God was
most wondrous wise,
When He created
Father's eyes.

For in them we find
a haven of peace,
Everlasting love
for children to keep.

Terry Yannetti

Unseen by either of us, Father
had appeared in the doorway.
"Give the child to me, Corrie," he said.
Father held the baby close, his white
beard brushing its cheek,
looking into the little face with eyes
as blue and innocent as the baby's...
"You say we could lose our lives for
this child. I would consider that the
greatest honor that could come
to my family."

CORRIE TEN BOOM